Rama and Sita

A Hindu Tale

Retold by Anita Ganeri
Illustrated by Adrija Ghosh

ISBN: 9781398377356

Hachette UK's policy is to use papers that are natural, renewable and recyclable products and made from wood grown in well-managed forests and other controlled sources. The logging and manufacturing processes are expected to conform to the environmental regulations of the country of origin.

Text © Anita Ganeri
Design, illustrations and layout © 2023 Hodder & Stoughton Limited
First published in 2023 by Hodder & Stoughton Limited (for its Hodder Education imprint, part of the Hodder Education Group),
An Hachette UK Company
Carmelite House, 50 Victoria Embankment, London EC4Y 0DZ

www.hoddereducation.com

Impression number 10 9 8 7 6 5 4 3 2 1
Year 2027 2026 2025 2024 2023

Author: Anita Ganeri
Series Editor: Catherine Coe
Commissioning Editor: Hamish Baxter
Illustrator: Adrija Ghosh
Educational reviewer: Pauline Allen
Design and layout: Helen Townson
Editorial: Amy Tyrer, Gaelle Lefevre

With thanks to Oxford Centre for Hindu Studies for expert information and advice.

With thanks to the schools that took part in the development of *Reading Planet* KS2, including: Ancaster CE Primary School, Ancaster; Downsway Primary School, Reading; Ferry Lane Primary School, London; Foxborough Primary School, Slough; Griffin Park Primary School, Blackburn; St Barnabas CE First & Middle School, Pershore; Tranmoor Primary School, Doncaster; and Wilton CE Primary School, Wilton.

The publishers would like to thank the following for permission to reproduce copyright material.

Cover and internals © ARTvektor/stock.adobe.com; p45, p46 © Dmitry Rukhlenko/stock.adobe.com; p47 left © WONG SZE FEI/stock.adobe.com; p47 right © Pavel/stock.adobe.com

All rights reserved. Apart from any use permitted under UK copyright law, no part of this publication may be reproduced or transmitted in any form or by any means, electronic or mechanical, including photocopying and recording, or held within any information storage and retrieval system, without permission in writing from the publisher or under licence from the Copyright Licensing Agency Limited. Further details of such licences (for reprographic reproduction) may be obtained from the Copyright Licensing Agency Limited, https://www.cla.co.uk/

A catalogue record for this title is available from the British Library.

Printed in India.

Orders: Please contact Hachette UK Distribution, Hely Hutchinson Centre, Milton Road, Didcot, Oxfordshire, OX11 7HH.

Telephone: (44) 01235 400555. Email: primary@hachette.co.uk

Contents

1. The Story Begins 6
2. A Difficult Decision 12
3. Life in the Forest 17
4. The Search for Sita 25
5. The Battle Begins 33
6. Going Home 42

What Is Hinduism? 45

Meet the Main Characters

The royal family

Dasaratha (say: *Daa-SHAARaa-taa*) King of Kosala

Kausalya (say: *Kaw-SHAA-ee-yaa*) the king's first wife; Rama's mother

Sumitra (say: *Suh-MIT-raa*) the king's middle wife; mother of twins, Lakshmana and Satrughna

Kaikeyi (say: *Kaiy-KAY-ee*) the king's youngest wife; Bharata's mother

Rama (say: *RAA-mah*) Dasaratha's eldest son, and heir

Lakshmana (say: *LUK-shmun-aa*) Satrughna's twin brother; Rama's brother and close companion

Dasaratha

Rama

Bharata (say: *BHU-rut-uh*) Rama's youngest brother

Satrughna (say: *Sha-TROO-gh-naa*) Lakshmana's twin brother and Bharata's close companion

Janaka (say: *JAA-nuh-kuh*) King of Mithila; father of Sita

Sita

Hanuman

Sugriva

Sita (say: *SEE-taa*) Rama's wife; daughter of King Janaka

Hanuman (say: *Hun-uh-MAAN*) monkey; son of the god of the wind

Sugriva (say: *Sug-REEV-uh*) King of the monkeys

Jambavan (say: *JAAM-bhuh-vaan*) King of the bears

The demons

Ravana (say: *Ruh-vuh-NAA*) King of the demons and ruler of Lanka

Indrajit (say: *IND-ruh-jit*) Ravana's son

Surpanakha (say: *Shur-PAH-nuh-kuh*) Ravana's sister

Ravana

1
The Story Begins

Long ago, a king called Dasaratha ruled the kingdom of Kosala in India. The king was a wise and fair leader. Under his rule, Kosala grew wealthy and powerful. Its people were happy and healthy, and lived in peace.

The capital city of Kosala was Ayodhya. There, King Dasaratha lived in a luxurious palace, built on top of a hill. Ayodhya sat on the banks of a river, and had flower-filled gardens and wide streets. It was a wonderful place to live. Boats sailed up and down the river. Chariots rattled along the streets. Merchants came from far and wide to buy and sell goods, while brave warriors kept the city safe.

The king had three beautiful wives – Queen Kausalya, Queen Sumitra and Queen Kaikeyi. He was rich beyond anyone's wildest dreams. Even so, he was still not happy because he did not have any children to leave his kingdom to when he died. He decided to do something about it, so he called for a priest.

"I must have a son," the king told the priest. "For the kingdom's sake."

"Very well, your majesty," the priest replied. "We will make an offering to the gods."

The priest lit a sacred fire by the river. He chanted hymns and prayers. He poured butter and flowers into the flames. Suddenly, a gigantic man, dressed in red, appeared from the flames. In his hands he held a gleaming golden bowl with a silver lid. It was filled with steaming, milky rice.

"The great god, Vishnu, has sent me to bring you this magical food," he said. "If your wives eat it, you will have four strong sons."

The giant handed the bowl to the astonished king, and disappeared back into the fire.

The next spring, four bouncing baby boys were born. Queen Kausalya gave birth to Rama; Queen Sumitra had twins, Lakshmana and Satrughna; and Queen Kaikeyi had Bharata. The king's dream had come true.

When the news was announced in the city, people were overjoyed. They sang and danced in the streets. They threw flower petals into the air.

To celebrate, the king opened up his treasure house. He ordered his servants to hand out gifts of money and jewels to the people.

The four boys grew up fast, learning all the skills they needed to be royal princes. They rode horses and elephants. They hunted, and shot bows and arrows. They studied the holy books. And, whatever they did, they were always together. Wherever Rama went, Lakshmana followed – he would not eat or sleep without Rama. Likewise, Lakshmana's twin brother, Satrughna, never left Bharata's side.

King Dasaratha loved all four of his sons, but Rama was his favourite. From birth, the gods had blessed Rama, and marked him out for greatness. When the king looked at him, he wanted to burst with pride. One day, when the princes were around 16 years old, a great holy man came to the palace. The king welcomed him warmly.

"Whatever you need, you shall have it," the king said. "You have my word."

"Your Majesty," replied the holy man, with a bow. "Evil demons have attacked the forest I live in. Soon, they will spread their wickedness far and wide across the world. There is only one man who can defeat them – your son, Rama. Please let him come with me for ten days."

"But Rama is so young …" the king began, frowning.

"Don't worry," the holy man told him. "The gods are looking down on Rama – he won't come to any harm."

Later that day, Rama and Lakshmana set off from Ayodhya with the holy man. They crossed over the river, and came to a deep, dark forest, where strange cries filled the air.

"This was a peaceful place," the holy man said, sadly, "until the demons came."

He led them to a clearing, where his small, wooden hut stood. There, he taught Rama some magic spells.

"When you chant these words," he told Rama, "the gods will send you weapons more powerful than any other weapons known on Earth. For now, be careful – the demons could attack at any time."

For six days and nights, Rama and Lakshmana kept guard outside the holy man's hut. They did not spot any demons.

Then, suddenly, the air became dark and cold. Two shrieking shapes swooped down from the sky. The demons flew straight at Rama. Rama called for the gods' magic weapons, and hurled them at the demons. Both demons fell from the sky, dead.

The forest was saved.

Rama asked the holy man what to do next.

"The King of Mithila has invited me to a great festival," the holy man replied. "Mithila's a city in the neighbouring kingdom. The king owns a mighty bow, which I think you might like to see."

When they reached Mithila, the king was delighted to show off his bow.

"The gods gave me this bow many years ago," he told them. "But it's so heavy that no one has ever been able to lift it. You can try if you like, Prince Rama. If you can fire the bow, you may marry my beautiful daughter, Sita. If she agrees, of course!"

Eagerly, Rama stepped forward. Without any trouble, he picked up the bow and fired it. The king couldn't believe his eyes.

Sita agreed to marry Rama, and soon afterwards, Rama's father and brothers arrived for the wedding.

And what a wedding it was! Not only did Sita marry Rama, but her sister married Lakshmana. One of her cousins married Bharata, and the other cousin married Satrughna. The celebrations lasted for days.

Then, all the brothers returned to Ayodhya, with their new wives.

2
A Difficult Decision

King Dasaratha ruled Kosala for many years, but he was getting old. It was time to hand his kingdom over to his eldest son. Everybody loved Rama, who was kind and wise, and always did his best for the people.

The king informed his ministers and holy men what he had decided. Then he called for Rama.

"I am old, my son. My hair is white, and I am so very tired," he said. "I want to make you king, but there's no time to lose. You will be crowned tomorrow."

News of Rama's coronation spread through the city like wildfire. People cheered, and chanted Rama's name. Colourful flags fluttered from buildings and flowers filled the streets. Music rang out from every house.

Everyone was delighted … well, almost everyone. Queen Kaikeyi, Rama's stepmother, was furious when she heard the news. She had always wanted her own son, Bharata, to be king. Kaikeyi thought quickly – she needed to get King Dasaratha to change his mind.

Cunning Queen Kaikeyi ran to her rooms in the palace, and threw herself on her bed, sobbing.

A worried servant went to fetch the king.

"What is wrong, my dear?" the king asked his wife, gently. "Are you ill, or has someone upset you? Tell me what will make you happy again."

The queen stopped crying, and looked up.

"You won't like it, my Lord," she said in a quiet voice.

"Ask me anything," the king said. "Anything."

"Long ago, I saved your life in battle. Do you remember?" Kaikeyi said. "You granted me two wishes in return."

"I remember," the king murmured, with a worried frown.

"I want you to grant the wishes now. First, I want you to make my son, Bharata, king. Second, I want you to send Rama away, to live in the forest for 14 years."

The king begged Kaikeyi to change her mind, but the queen refused. He could not go back on his word, so he called for Rama, and told him to leave Ayodhya.

"Don't be sad, Father," Rama said. "I will gladly do as you wish. It is my duty."

He went to tell Sita and Lakshmana.

"I'm coming with you," Sita told him.

"Me too," said Lakshmana.

Lakshmana said a sad goodbye to his wife, who was staying behind in the palace. Then, the three packed a few belongings, got into their chariot, and drove quickly out of the city gates. They did not dare to look back.

In the palace, the king lay in his bed, tears streaming down his cheeks. No one was able to comfort him – his grief was so great.

"Oh, Rama," he cried out, pitifully. "How shall I live without you?"

And in the night, the king died.

Ayodhya was filled with sadness at the king's death. The streets lay silent and empty, and no one sang or danced any more.

When Bharata was told about his father's death, he rushed to the palace. His mother, Queen Kaikeyi, came to greet him.

"My son," she said. "Now that your father is dead, and Rama has gone, you will be king. Be happy. I have done all of this for you."

"What have you done?" Bharata cried. "I don't want to be king. The throne belongs to Rama, and I am loyal to him. I will go and bring him home."

So, Bharata set out with a huge army of soldiers, horses and elephants. They spent days and nights in the forest, searching for Rama.

One day, Bharata spotted smoke rising among the trees. He found Rama with Sita and Lakshmana, sitting by a campfire in a forest clearing. Bharata told them about King Dasaratha's death, and begged Rama to come back with him.

"I must stay here and obey our father's wishes," Rama said. "Go back to Ayodhya, and rule in my place until I come home."

"Very well," said Bharata, sadly. "But give me a pair of your sandals. I will put them in your place on the throne, until you return."

3
Life in the Forest

When Bharata had gone, Rama, Sita and Lakshmana left their camp and went deeper into the forest. They needed to find somewhere to live while they were away. But the further they went into the forest, the darker and gloomier it grew.

They followed the river to a mountain, and came to a hut where a holy man lived. Rama asked the holy man if he knew of any suitable places to live nearby.

"I will gladly show you," the holy man said. "But first, please give me your bow."

Rama handed over his bow. The holy man took it and disappeared into his hut. When he came out, he had a different bow in his hand, made from gold and diamonds, and glinting in the sun.

"Take this bow," he told Rama. "It fell from heaven, many years ago, and will keep you safe. An arrow fired from this bow will never miss its target."

The next morning, the holy man took Rama to the top of the mountain, from where they could see the enormous forest stretched below.

The holy man pointed out a path to Rama. It snaked down the mountain and through the trees.

"Follow that path," he told Rama. "It will lead you to a peaceful spot by a stream. But be careful. Beyond the edge of the forest and over the sea lies the kingdom of Lanka. It is ruled by Ravana, the evil demon king. He is terrifying to look at, with ten heads and eyes as red as blood. Although Lanka is far away, his demons are taking over the forest. Be on your guard, especially at night."

The path was tough going for the three travellers. They tripped over tangled branches and stumbled on the uneven ground. Their clothes were ripped by sharp thorns. At last, they reached a beautiful clearing in the forest, next to a rippling stream.

"This is the place the holy man told me about," said Rama. "We can stay here for a while."

Quickly, Lakshmana set to work building a hut from mud and leaves for Rama and Sita. Then he built one for himself.

The days passed by peacefully, and Rama, Sita and Lakshmana settled into forest life. Every morning, they bathed in the stream. Every evening, they sat by the campfire and told stories. They tried not to think too much about home.

One day, they heard a loud rustling, and a foul-looking creature stepped out of the trees. The creature was half-person, half-monster, with warty, yellow skin and claws on its fingers and toes.

They gasped in horror. Then, Rama took charge and stood up.

"I am Rama," he said, politely. "This is Sita, my wife, and Lakshmana, my brother."

"And I am Surpanakha," cackled the creature, "the sister of King Ravana. I want you to be my husband, Rama. We are meant to be together. We'll leave this place and live in Lanka, in luxury."

"But I'm already married," said Rama, with a smile.

"Then I shall marry *you*," hissed Surpanakha, turning to Lakshmana.

"I'm married, too," replied Lakshmana.

Surpanakha howled in anger. She glared at Sita.

"This is all your fault," she screamed.

In a fury, Surpanakha charged at Sita, sharp claws at the ready. Quick as a flash, Rama and Lakshmana grabbed Surpanakha and flung her high over the treetops and far away from their camp.

Some way away, Surpanakha's cousin, General Khara, was pitching camp in the forest with his demon army. Weeping and wailing, Surpanakha crawled up to his camp.

"Help me! Help me!" she screeched. "I've been attacked!"

Khara listened to Surpanakha's story. Then, he summoned fourteen thousand demons, and flew off to take revenge.

But even such a huge and hideous army was no match for Rama's and Lakshmana's skills. In a flash, the two brothers killed every one of the demons, including General Khara himself.

Surpanakha looked on in horror. Then, she hurried off to Lanka to tell her brother, Ravana, what had happened.

Ravana sat on his great throne, each of his ten faces looking like thunder.

"Who did this?" he hissed.

"Rama, son of King Dasaratha," she whined.

"Rama?" asked Ravana. "And how big was his army?"

"There was no army, brother," replied Surpanakha. "Rama and his brother, Lakshmana, killed them all."

"Pah!" roared Ravana. "Well, I'll have to teach this Rama a lesson."

"You don't know him," his sister sneered. "He is the greatest warrior ever seen."

"So, what do you suggest I do, sister?" Ravana said, exploding with rage. "If you're so clever …"

"Well," said Surpanakha. "There is one thing … Rama lives in the forest with his wife, Sita, and his brother, Lakshmana. Sita is very beautiful and kind, and Rama loves her more than anything in the world. He could not live without her."

"Then I'll go to the forest and kidnap her," smirked Ravana. "I'll bring her back here, and if she's as beautiful as you say, I'll marry her myself."

"But Rama and Lakshmana will never let you near her," said his sister. "Your only chance to succeed is if you get her on her own."

"Dear sister, don't worry," cackled Ravana. "I have an idea."

Ravana called for Maricha, the magician, and told him what he was planning to do. Maricha was horrified.

"I beg you not to do this, my Lord," Maricha said. "Rama has the gods on his side. He will never let you take Sita. He will kill you and destroy your kingdom."

"I want your magic," shouted Ravana, "not your advice. Come with me and help me. Or get out of my sight."

"As you wish, Majesty," Maricha agreed.

So, early the next morning, Ravana and Maricha went to the royal stables and picked out the finest horses and chariot. Then, they sped away across the ocean in search of Sita.

Sometime later, Ravana's chariot landed in the forest, close to Rama's hut. The chariot was hidden from sight by the trees.

"Now, work your magic," Ravana hissed to Maricha.

Maricha clapped his hands and turned into a dazzling, golden deer. It wasn't long before Sita spotted it among the trees. She asked Rama to catch it for her – it was the most beautiful creature she had ever seen.

"Stay here with Sita," Rama told Lakshmana, picking up his bow.

Rama set off after the deer, which led him deeper and deeper into the forest. Finally, he got close enough to shoot. The arrow hit the deer in its side. It fell to the ground, and turned back into Maricha, the magician.

Mimicking Rama's voice, Maricha cried out:

"Help me! Oh, dearest Sita, help me! I'm hurt!"

In the distance, Sita and Lakshmana heard the cry for help. They thought that it was Rama – it sounded just like him.

"Rama is hurt," Sita said. "You must go and help him, Lakshmana."

"But I promised to stay and look after you," Lakshmana replied.

"Don't you care if he dies?" said Sita.

"Very well," sighed Lakshmana. "I'll go."

From his hiding place, Ravana watched as Lakshmana set off to help Rama. He put on some ragged, orange robes to disguise himself as a poor holy man, and hobbled to Sita's door. Sita was surprised to see a stranger in the clearing, but he looked old and harmless. So, she gave him a seat and brought him some food and water.

"I am Sita," she said. "My husband is Prince Rama. Who are you?"

All at once, the birds stopped singing, and the forest went deathly quiet. The stranger clapped his hands and his rags fell away, revealing a terrible demon with ten heads and twenty arms.

"I am Ravana, King of the demons," he boomed, "and ruler of Lanka. Forget about Prince Rama. Come with me, and be my queen."

"Never!" said Sita, shaking with fear.

But Ravana dragged Sita to his chariot and sped off. As they flew over the forest, Sita spied two monkeys sitting on a rock, far below. She took off her necklace and bracelets, wrapped them in her silk scarf and dropped them down to the monkeys.

4
The Search for Sita

Meanwhile, in the forest, Rama realised that he had been tricked. He raced back home to make sure Sita was safe.

On the way, he met Lakshmana who told him that Sita was gone.

"The demons have taken her," cried Rama, in dismay.

"We will find her," said Lakshmana, "and bring her back."

Bows in hand, the brothers set off to search for Sita.

Suddenly, they came upon the great vulture king, Jayatu. He was lying on the ground, badly injured.

"Prince Rama," murmured Jayatu. "Sita is alive. But the demon king, Ravana, has taken her. I saw him and tried my best to stop him, but he was too strong for me."

"Where has he taken her?" asked Rama.

"South," Jayatu whispered. "Towards Lanka."

And then Jayatu died.

So, Rama and Lakshmana headed south. Soon, they reached a sparkling blue lake, filled with lotus flowers. An old woman lived by the lakeside, and she came out to greet them. She told them that she had seen Ravana and Sita, a few days ago.

"We'll never catch up with them now," Rama sighed, sadly.

"Don't despair," replied the old woman, pointing to a nearby hill. "Two monkeys live on that hill. One is Sugriva, King of the monkeys. The other is Hanuman, son of the god of the wind. They will help you find Sita."

Far away, Ravana reached Lanka. He showed Sita his sumptuous palace, and boasted about how rich he was.

"Marry me," he hissed, "and all of this will be yours!"

"Marry you?" sobbed Sita. "Never. You are a monster."

"You have a year to change your mind," growled Ravana. "Until then, you'll be my prisoner. Guards, take her away."

After saying goodbye to the old woman, Rama and Lakshmana climbed the hill to find the monkeys. They told the monkeys what had happened.

Sugriva listened thoughtfully, then he disappeared into his cave. He brought out a small package, wrapped in a silk scarf, and handed it to Rama.

"A few days ago, we saw a princess being carried south by Ravana," Sugriva told them. "As they flew over us, she threw this down."

Rama opened the parcel, and gazed at the cluster of sparkling jewels inside.

"These belong to Sita," he said, sadly.

"We will help you find her and defeat Ravana," said Sugriva. "But we need to be quick. Ravana is powerful and evil, and will stop at nothing."

At once, Sugriva summoned a huge army of monkeys – the biggest ever seen. From all four corners of the world, they swarmed to the mountain to join Sugriva.

Jambavan, the King of the bears, sent thousands of bears to fight alongside the monkeys.

Sugriva stood in front of the soldiers.

"Search every forest, valley and hillside for Sita," he told them. "Search every river, lake and sea."

Then, he called for Hanuman.

"Hanuman," Sugriva continued. "You are my bravest and most loyal friend. You will head south to Lanka, with Jambavan."

Before Hanuman left, Rama gave him a precious gold ring.

"Take this gold ring to Sita," he said. "Her father gave it to me and had my name written on it. Sita will know at once that it is mine, and that we are looking for her."

Hanuman and Jambavan headed south, until they came to the very tip of India and the vast ocean beyond. Out in the distance, they could see a tiny black dot of land – Lanka. But they were filled with despair. They had searched high and low across India for Sita, but couldn't find her anywhere. Glumly, they sat down on the shore, and gazed out to sea.

A huge vulture perched nearby. It hadn't eaten for several days, and thought that a monkey or two would make a tasty meal.

"A brave vulture once gave its life for Rama," said Hanuman, spotting the ragged old bird.

The vulture hopped down from its perch and shuffled towards them.

"That was my brother," the vulture said. "How do you know about him?"

Hanuman told the vulture about the search for Rama's wife, Sita.

"This time, I will help you," said the vulture. "I saw Ravana fly this way, carrying a young woman. He was heading to Lanka."

"How far is Lanka?" Hanuman asked, leaping to his feet.

"It's that island over there," the vulture replied.

Hanuman peered across the water. He could just make out the tiny dot. But how were they going to get across the sea and back again?

"You are the son of the wind god," the vulture reminded him. "You are the only one that can leap so far. You must go, and bring back news of Sita."

Leaving Jambavan on the shore, Hanuman climbed a nearby hill. He grew bigger and bigger until he reached a gigantic size. He stretched out his tail, crouched down low and took a deep breath.

Then he took a giant leap, up into the sky, and out across the sea.

Hanuman soared high over the ocean. Further and further he flew, until he spotted the forests and rivers of Lanka far below. Landing on a hillside, he crept towards the city, and hid until it got dark. He did not want to be seen by the guards.

When it was dark, Hanuman shrank down to the size of a cat. He slipped into the city and made his way to Ravana's palace. It was an astonishing sight, with walls of solid gold and golden domes on its roofs. Even the gravel on the garden paths was made of specks of ground-up jewels.

Hanuman searched for Sita in every room, and in every park and alleyway in the city. Just as he was about to give up, he spotted a beautiful garden, blooming with flowers and trees. Hanuman climbed the tallest tree and hid among its branches. On the ground below sat a woman with torn clothes and eyes that were red from crying. Hanuman knew at once that it was Sita.

Hanuman did not want to frighten Sita by calling out. He softly whispered Rama's name. Sita looked up and saw Hanuman in the tree.

"Who are you?" she asked, quietly. "How do you know my husband's name?"

"I am Hanuman, son of the wind god, and Rama's faithful friend," replied Hanuman. "He sent me to find you."

"Why should I believe you?" said Sita. "This could be a trick."

"I will show you," said Hanuman.

He gave Rama's gold ring to Sita.

"I know this ring," she said, gazing at it. "Oh, Hanuman, thank you. In return, please take this jewel to him, to prove that I am alive."

She gave Hanuman a large, sparkling jewel.

"I must go now," said Hanuman. "But Rama will come with his army to rescue you."

He scurried back through the city, and climbed the hill again. Once more, he leapt across the ocean. Then, he and Jambavan hurried back to where Rama was waiting.

5
The Battle Begins

Rama was overjoyed to hear Hanuman's news and to see Sita's jewel.

"We must go to Lanka at once," he said.

"Jump on my back," said Hanuman.

So, Rama set off with Hanuman, Sugriva, Jambavan, and their great army of monkeys and bears. Day and night they marched, until they reached the sea.

"How are we going to get across?" asked Lakshmana, peering across the water.

"We will build a bridge," Rama replied.

For the next five days, the monkeys and bears collected rocks and trees from the hills to build a fine, wide bridge across the sea. Rama and Lakshmana led the army across, and set up camp on a hill outside Ravana's city.

Ravana had spies, who brought the king news of Rama's arrival in Lanka. Ravana told his best and most blood-thirsty demon soldiers to prepare for battle.

The next day, Rama led his army into the city.

"Let the battle begin!" he cried.

Armed with rocks and tree trunks, the monkeys and bears charged. Facing them were hundreds of thousands of demons, carrying axes and swords. The two sides fought fiercely, and by evening, thousands of demons lay dead.

It looked as if Rama's army was winning, so Ravana sent his son, Indrajit, to fight Rama. Indrajit could make himself invisible.

Unseen by Rama and Lakshmana, Indrajit fired arrow after arrow at them. As the arrows hit their targets, they turned into deadly snakes. The snakes wound their coils around and around Rama and Lakshmana, tighter and tighter, until the brothers could hardly move or breathe.

Thinking that Rama and Lakshmana were dead, Indrajit flew back to tell Ravana. But Rama and Lakshmana were not finished yet. Suddenly, a storm blew up and lightning flashed across the sky. A great eagle swooped down. At once, the startled snakes let go of Rama and Lakshmana, and slithered away in fear.

"You have saved our lives," croaked Rama.

"You are welcome," replied the eagle. "Now, go and save Sita."

The eagle spread out his mighty wings, and flew back up into the clouds.

When Ravana heard that Rama was still alive, he exploded in rage. He sent his bravest generals into battle, but Rama and his army killed every one of them, or chased them away.

"There's nothing else for it," cried Ravana. "I'll have to go myself."

Ravana leapt into his chariot and set off for the battlefield, holding a weapon in each of his twenty arms. Surely, he would be too strong for Rama? But Rama smashed Ravana's chariot into pieces, and tossed his weapons to the ground. Ravana waited for Rama to kill him.

"I will spare your life this time," Rama told him. "But come back, when you dare. I will be waiting for you."

Still Ravana would not give up, and instead he thought up a cunning plan. He sent his servants to fetch his brother, Kumbhakarna.

"Rama won't stand a chance against *him*!" he cackled.

Kumbhakarna was no ordinary demon – he was a monster who lived in a huge, golden mansion, deep under the ground. He had an enormous appetite, and gobbled up so much food that he'd grown to a giant size. Luckily, he spent most of his time asleep and he didn't like to be woken up.

The servants found Kumbhakarna lying on his giant bed, snoring loudly. They tried everything to wake him. They banged drums, rang bells, beat him and poked him with sticks. But still, he snoozed and snored. Next, they sent hundreds of elephants to trample over him, and, at last, he opened his eyes.

"Who dares to wake me up?" he snarled.

"Lanka is in danger, my Lord," the servants told him. "King Ravana needs your help."

Heaving himself out of bed, Kumbhakarna lumbered slowly over to Ravana's palace. Ravana told him what he needed him to do.

"Don't worry," Kumbhakarna told Ravana, grinning and licking his lips. "What can this Rama do to me? He might be a great warrior, but he won't be able to touch me. I'll kill him and eat him! Then, Lanka will be safe."

With one giant stride, Kumbhakarna stepped over the city walls and into battle. The ground shook under his feet. Thousands of monkeys and bears tried to stop him. They hurled rocks and trees at him, but he simply tossed them away. They tried to bite and scratch him, but he picked them up and threw them aside.

When none of that worked, Hanuman struck a gigantic boulder, the size of a mountain at Kumbhakarna, while Lakshmana shot hundreds of arrows at him. Kumbhakarna stumbled, but still he did not fall down.

Kumbhakarna was furious. He was also hungry, which made him even more dangerous. He wanted to get the battle over so that he could return to his mansion for some food.

"Where are you, Rama?" he screamed. "Show yourself, if you dare."

"I'm here," said Rama, appearing over the top of the hill.

"Are you ready to die?"

Kumbhakarna, holding a deadly club in his hand, charged at Rama.

But Rama was ready for him. He placed a golden arrow on to his bow, took careful aim, and fired. With a colossal crash, Kumbhakarna fell to the ground. As Rama and his army watched, the monster's massive body rolled down the hill, into the sea, and sank beneath the waves.

Ravana's sons came to see him in his palace. They told him what had happened.

"It's over," Ravana sighed. "The battle is over."

"Don't give up now, Father," they replied. "We will fight for you."

One by one, Ravana's sons went into battle, and one by one, they were killed. Soon, only Indrajit was left, and he got ready to fight Rama again.

"Don't go," begged Ravana. "I don't want to lose you, too."

"This time, I will kill him, Father," said Indrajit. "I will take revenge for my uncle and brothers."

Indrajit leapt into his flame-red chariot, pulled by four tigers. He made himself invisible, and flew over the battlefield. Then, he began shooting arrows at Rama's army, thousands and thousands at a time, hitting countless bears and monkeys. Rama and Lakshmana fell to the ground, too, both badly injured. Gleefully, Indrajit went back to his father.

Among the wounded was Jambavan, King of the bears. He called for Hanuman.

"Listen carefully," he whispered. "Only you can save us. Far away in the Himalayas, there is a mountain where magical herbs grow. These herbs can heal wounds, mend broken bones, and even bring the dead back to life. Go quickly, and bring the herbs back."

As fast as the wind, Hanuman flew over rivers, forests, cities and plains to the Himalayas, but he did not know which herbs to pick. So, he tore the whole mountain from the ground, and carried it back to Lanka. There, the sweet smell of the herbs wafted over the battlefield and worked their magic. Before long, Rama, Lakshmana and all of the fallen soldiers were brought back to life and good health. Afterwards, Hanuman put the mountain back in its rightful place.

Howling with fury, Indrajit hid in his father's palace, but Lakshmana soon tracked him down and killed him.

Ravana's last and favourite son was gone, so it was time for Ravana to face Rama alone. He called for his finest black steel armour and a helmet for each of his heads. Then, he swept out of the palace.

"It is time for Rama and his wretched brother to meet their end," he shrieked at his generals. "They have taken my sons, and I will show them no mercy. Tell the army to follow me."

Then, with a blood-curdling cry, he got into his chariot, loaded with deadly weapons of all kinds, and set off to find Rama.

Rama was ready for him. The two circled around each other, and hurled weapons back and forth. Ravana shot at Rama with arrows tipped with animal heads that had sharp, biting teeth. Rama shot at Ravana with arrows of fire, which exploded as they landed. The battle grew fiercer and fiercer – neither one of them would give up.

After many days and nights of fighting, it was finally time to bring the battle to an end. Rama picked up the deadly bow and arrow that the wise man had given him – the one that never missed its target. Now was its time to strike. Carefully, Rama drew the bow, and fired. The arrow flew like a flame through the air, straight and true, and struck Ravana in the middle of his chest, straight in his heart.

With a terrible shriek, the evil demon king toppled out of his chariot, dead.

The battle was over. Ravana was dead, and his evil reign at an end. The sound of cheering filled Lanka, as the monkeys and bears rejoiced. Rama turned his thoughts to Sita. He had missed her so much, and longed to see her again.

6
Going Home

Rama sent Hanuman to the garden where Sita was being kept prisoner, to tell her the good news. Sita was delighted – she couldn't wait to see Rama again. A little while later, Rama and Sita were reunited, and promised never to be parted again.

A message arrived from Ayodhya. With evil Ravana gone for good, it was time for Rama and Sita to go home. The 14 years were not over, but Bharata could not wait – he wanted Rama to be king. Rama went to say goodbye to all the monkeys, Jambavan, the bear king, and Sugriva and Hanuman.

"Go back and rule your kingdoms," he told them. "I can never thank you enough for all you have done for us."

But they did not want to leave him.

"We will come with you," Hanuman said, with a smile. "We want to see you crowned. After that, we will go home."

So, Rama, Sita and Lakshmana travelled back to Ayodhya with their friends. They rode in a glittering, golden chariot, in the shape of a gigantic swan.

When Bharata heard that Rama had arrived, he was overjoyed. He took Rama's old sandals from the throne, and went to greet his brother with Rama's mother, Queen Kausalya, by his side.

"I have looked after the kingdom for you," he said. "Now it is yours at last."

He put the sandals on Rama's feet.

A few days later, Rama and Sita were crowned. The celebrations were the greatest that the city had ever seen. Once more, there was singing and dancing. Once more, flags fluttered from the buildings, and brightly coloured ribbons and lanterns hung from the trees. Crowds of people lined the streets to catch a glimpse of their new king and queen.

"King Rama! Queen Sita!" they shouted. "Long live the king and queen."

And so, Rama and Sita's reign began. It was a happy time for everyone. No one went hungry or fell ill, and no one was lonely or sad. For the people of the kingdom of Kosala, Rama was their perfect king.

What Is Hinduism?

A Hindu story

Rama and Sita is based on a well-known story from the religion of Hinduism.

What is Hinduism?

Hinduism is a religion which began in India at least 4,500 years ago. Its followers are called Hindus. Most of the world's Hindus live in India, but there are also Hindu communities in other places, such as the United Kingdom and North America.

What is the Hindu view of the world?

There are many different ways of being a Hindu, but most Hindus share the same basic ways of seeing things. They see that there is a great spirit or force, called Brahman, at work in the world. Some Hindus call Brahman 'God'. Hindus worship Brahman in many forms – some male and some female. Each form stands for a different part of Brahman, and is often represented as a god or goddess. Rama is a form of the god, Vishnu, but is also seen as a god in his own right. In their everyday lives, Hindus advocate working hard, telling the truth, and looking after their family. They think that every living thing has a soul and that all life should be respected. When you die, your soul is born again in another body. Your next life depends on how you behave in your current life.

Who and where do Hindus worship?

Many Hindus worship in a mandir, or temple. There is no set day for worship. Some Hindus go to the mandir every day; others may only go at special times, such as for festivals.

Each mandir is dedicated to a particular god, goddess or holy person. Their image stands in the most sacred part of the mandir. It is looked after by a priest. Worshippers come to see the sacred image. They say prayers and chant verses from the sacred text. They also make offerings of flowers, fruit and sweets to the image. In return, they hope to receive the gods' blessing.

Hindus also worship at home. They may have a special room set aside for worship, or a corner of a room or a shelf where a sacred image stands.

What are the sacred books of Hinduism?

In Hinduism, there are lots of different sacred books. The story of Rama and Sita comes from the Ramayana. It is a very long poem, made up of 24,000 verses. It was composed around 4,000 years ago, but was not written down until much later. It is still very popular today. In India, people can read the story in comic books, see it acted out in plays and watch it on television.

What does this story mean to Hindus?

The story of Rama and Sita is very important to Hindus. Hindus believe that Rama is a form of the god Vishnu, sent down to earth to save it from evil. The main lesson of the Ramayana is the struggle between good (Rama) and evil (Ravana), with good winning in the end. But the poem also teaches about important values, such as love, loyalty and duty. Many Hindu festivals are based on the story of Rama and Sita. In March or April, Hindus mark Rama's birthday. In September, they remember Rama's victory over Ravana. The most important festival is Diwali. It takes place in October or November, and celebrates Rama and Sita's return to Ayodhya. Hindus decorate their homes and mandirs with little clay lamps, to guide and welcome Rama and Sita home.

Now answer the questions …

1 What was the capital city of Kosala?

2 'Rama called for the gods' magic weapons, and hurled them at the demons.' What is another word that could be used instead of 'hurled'?

3 Look at page 15. Why do you think the king died?

4 What happened on pages 22 to 24, when Ravana and Maricha landed in the forest?

5 What did you think would happen when Rama led his army into Ravana's city on page 33?

6 Why did Hanuman tear the whole mountain from the ground on page 40?

7 Look at page 41: 'Then, with a blood-curdling cry…' What does 'blood-curdling' mean?

8 Do you think King Dasaratha was right to send Rama away when Queen Kaikeyi told him it was one of her wishes? What would you have done?